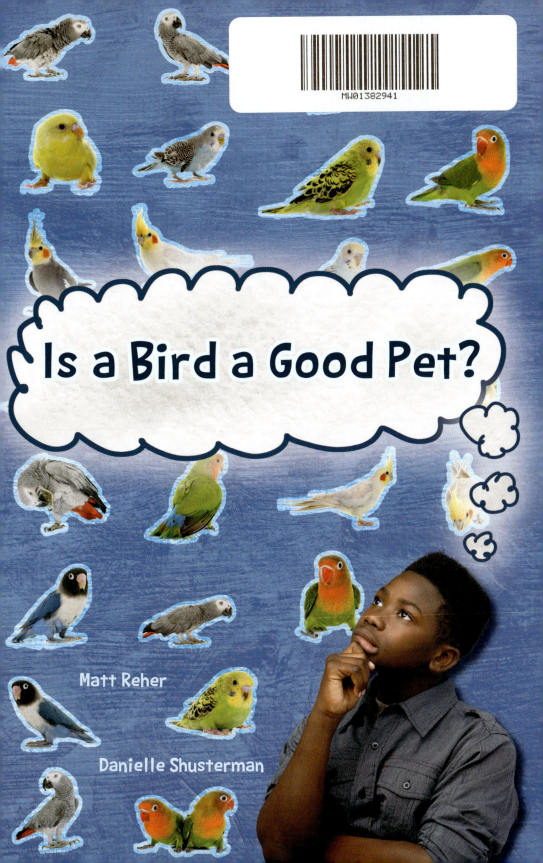

Is a Bird a Good Pet?

Matt Reher

Danielle Shusterman

I live here.

What pet do I want?

I want a bird.

Birds get bugs and seeds to eat. 7

My bird can't do that.

I have to get food for my bird.

Birds get water.

My bird can't do that.

I have to get water for my bird.

Birds like to play.

My bird can't do that.

I have to get toys for my bird.

Birds want to fly.

My bird will want to fly.

The cage has to be big.

22 Where will a big cage go?

It can't go in here.

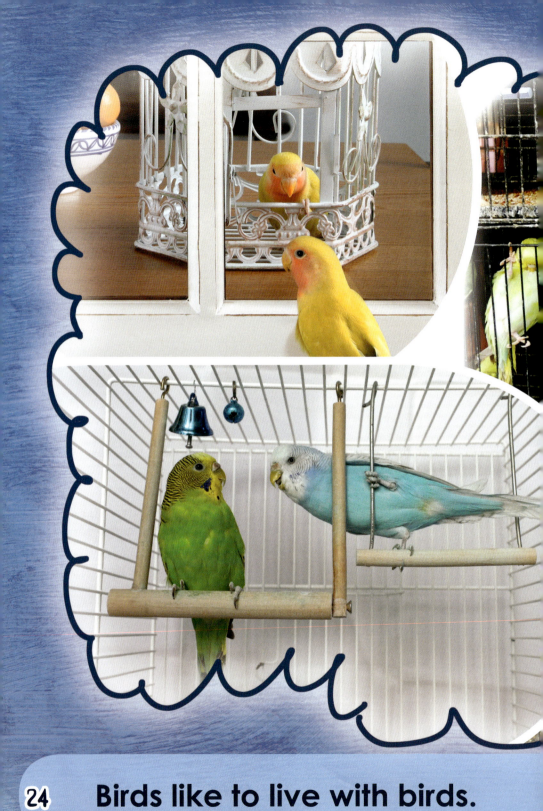

24 Birds like to live with birds.

Is a bird the one for me?

Birds want lots of stuff.

I will get a cat.